# I Love God—
# And My Husband

## Marion Stroud

Read this book on your own, or study and
discuss it in a group. A leader's guide with
hints and helps for a group study based
on this book is available from your local
bookstore or from Victor Books at $1.25.

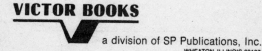
**VICTOR BOOKS**

a division of SP Publications, Inc.
WHEATON, ILLINOIS 60187

Originally published in 1973 in England as *I Love God and You*. American edition published by special arrangement with CPAS Publications, a department of the Church Pastoral Aid Society, London. Americanized for U.S. and Canadian readers.

*Second printing, 1976*

Unless otherwise stated, Bible quotations are from the *New American Standard Bible*, copyrighted by The Lockman Foundation. Other quotations are from the *Living Bible* (LB), copyrighted by Tyndale House Publishers, Wheaton, Illinois, and from the *New International Version of the New Testament,* (NIV) © 1973 by the New York Bible Society International. All Bible quotations are used with permission.

Copyright 1973, by Marion Stroud
Library of Congress Catalog Card Number: 76–8629
ISBN: 0-88207-734-1

VICTOR BOOKS
A division of SP Publications, Inc.
P.O. Box 1825 • Wheaton, Ill. 60187

# Contents

# Acknowledgments

This book is not the work of one person, but is based on the shared experiences of many women. The stories are about real people and are founded on fact, though names and details have been changed to spare them any embarrassment.

Many people have helped with this book. Some have prayed; others have shared in letters, tapes, and telephone calls what God has taught them; a few have met in my home to discuss the book chapter by chapter.

Three people have played a special part: my mother, who ran the house for a week when it seemed as if the last few chapters would never be written; Janet, who not only typed and retyped the manuscript, but also offered lots of wise advice and constructive criticism; and finally my husband. He gave me the man's-eye-view of many of the topics covered by the book, and cheerfully weathered the storms of authorship.

To each and every one of them I want to say "Thank you. Your help made the whole project possible."

MARION STROUD

# 1

# Let's Start at
# the Very Beginning

If you are perfectly content with the way you are living now and feel no need of any help outside yourself, then this book is not for you.

If you have never wondered what life is all about, or never wished that you could unravel the tangle of the past and start over again, then read no further. You see, God's offer of forgiveness and a purposeful, loving relationship with Himself can only be appreciated or accepted by those with a sense of need.

Take Jane for example. Jane first began to notice that life has problems when she was about 15. Her mother thought she was moody because she was a teenager; her father assumed she was worried about exams. Jane knew they were both wrong about that just like everything else. Once she got away from home and out of school she was certain that all her troubles would be over.

At first, the freedom of a job and an apartment which she shared with a co-worker was exhilarating. But soon the pressure started to build up as her friends began to flaunt their engagement rings. Freedom to do her own thing no longer seemed desirable.

However, before Jane could become too despondent along came Peter, and she heaved a sigh of relief. She was not on the shelf after all! Soon she was engaged, then married and living in a cozy efficiency apartment. Surely everything would be fine now. And it was . . . for a while.

Of course they only stayed in the apartment until they had saved up enough for a deposit on a house. Once they moved in, Jane just could not wait to leave her job—both her neighbors were pushing new and shiny baby carriages.

Jane had several children and gained more weight than she had bargained for. She was rather shattered to realize that being the ideal wife and mother so glowingly portrayed in women's magazines required more than the possession of husband and children! There were good days, of course, but then there were others, when life seemed to be an endless round of picking up toys and answering the same question for the hundredth time. Jane decided that what she really needed was a job or other outside interest to stretch her mind and brighten up her days.

At last the children were in school, and Jane found just the job she wanted. She had reached her goal, but the butterfly of happiness and fulfillment eluded her.

Like most of us, Jane did not want to admit her dissatisfaction to anyone else. For years she had been living in the future, reaching out for the next stage in life, certain that this would complete her happiness. But things had not turned out as she had planned.

Instead of being the perfect patient mother to clean, tidy, and obedient children, she found herself shouting impatiently at untidy, unruly brats who often compared her unfavorably with their teacher. She knew that many of her friends envied her happy marriage and interesting job, and yet she knew that they saw only the surface of her life. There were some things that she could not share even with Peter. There was an inner loneliness and restlessness she was unable to quell.

It was then that Jane stopped to think things out. What was the point of all her frantic activity? She had everything that was supposed to make life complete, yet nothing gave her the key to life itself. She took a good look at herself—and did not like what she saw. She had to admit that her troubles stemmed from inside herself, because the people and circumstances around her changed very little. So for months Jane tried to exercise her will power and change herself—without success. Nothing altered: the restlessness and dissatisfaction were still there and even got worse as time went on. Eventually she stopped trying and had to admit defeat. It was then, having reached rock-bottom, that Jane was ready to meet the one person who could transform her life—Jesus Christ.

We all have different goals in life and various ways of achieving them. Like Jane, many of us spend long years thinking that real satisfaction is just around the corner, and then find that we are no closer to our goal now than we were at the beginning. But there is good news for all rainbow-chasers. God loves individual men and women and offers the wonderful gift of a fresh start and a new life to everyone—on the one condition that we admit our need. Of course, we all hate having to admit that we have needs that we cannot meet, yet this is essential before those needs can be met. Having faced up to it, let's see how this change from the old life to the new can come about.

## In the Beginning

In the beginning God created men and women so they would live in a happy and loving relationship with Himself with a two-way traffic of love flowing between them. But because God did not want mere machines that did all the right things automatically, He gave people the ability to choose between good and evil, between going their own way or God's way. Men and women chose to go their own way. Thinking that they knew best, they decided to live as they pleased, and ignored God's purpose for their lives. It was not long before they discovered that life away from God was only half a life, but by then it was too late. The rebellion that has affected people all the way down through history had started.

The Bible calls turning one's back on God *sin*. Sin has formed a barrier between God and us, cutting us off from the kind of life God wants us to have—in touch with Himself. It makes no difference whether we have pleased ourselves rather than God in just one part of our lives or in each part. The sin barrier separates each person from God. We cannot tunnel our way through it by good resolutions, kind deeds, or an outward show of religion. The sin barrier stunts our lives, and we are stuck with it.

The next move had to be from God's side. Loving people as He does, He longed to set us free from the chains we forged for ourselves and yet being wholly just, He could not ignore the sin barrier. It had to be dealt with. Someone had to pay to have it removed. So Jesus came—God Himself in a human body—the perfect link between the two sides.

Jesus Christ was completely human. He knew what it was to work hard with His hands in a land occupied by enemy forces. He had few material possessions and no settled home life. He knew what it meant to be hungry, tired, and hounded by men who hated Him. Yet in spite of these outward circumstances, He showed how life is meant to be lived—full of love, joy, peace, and a freedom which nothing could destroy. Having lived a life that pleased God the Father in every respect, He allowed Himself to be crucified, the innocent willingly accepting the death penalty passed on the guilty. But the story does not end there. Death could not hold the Son of God captive. After three days he was more alive than ever, and is still alive today. God Himself did what we could not do. He Himself paid the price He had set and dealt with the barrier between us.

## Jesus' Gift
Now His gift of a past wiped clean and a present full of joy, purpose, and freedom to live as God intends is available to everyone. God longs for us to accept this gift, but He does not promise that our acceptance will insure us against all life's problems and difficulties. Nor will it turn us into perfect

people overnight. What He does promise is His help 'and company in every situation, and His power within us to change us just as much as we will allow Him to.

So far, we have seen that all the initiative has come from God's side. A new life and a fresh start are available as free gifts, but they are not ours until we take them. In our household, we get special offers and free gifts stuffed in our mailbox at least once a week. But they are worthless to me, unless I take them to the appropriate store and claim what is being offered. So how do we make the gift that God offers our own personal property? Let's take it step by step in order.

1. We admit that we have sinned and that there is nothing that we can do to change ourselves.

2. We believe that Jesus took our punishment, and that through what He has done alone, the barrier between God and ourselves has been removed.

3. We turn away from our old attitudes and actions, telling God that we are sorry for what we have done wrong in thought and deed, and asking for His forgiveness.

4. Then we hand over the control of our life to Jesus Christ, thanking Him for all that He did to make this fresh start possible, and asking Him to live out His life through us.

If you are ready to do this, perhaps you would like to pray this prayer or one like it in your own words, and start right now on your new life with God.

"Lord Jesus, I know that my life has fallen short of Your standards and that I am out of touch with You. I cannot change myself. I believe that

You took the punishment that I deserve, so that I can be forgiven and changed. Thank You for loving me so much. I am truly sorry for the past; please take over the controls of my life, and make me into the kind of person that You want me to be."

# 2

# Living

# and Learning

So now you have been adopted! That is, if you have taken up God's offer mentioned in chapter one. The Bible says that when you become a Christian, you are adopted into the Christian family. God is your Father; you can share all your joys and problems with Him, and He can be trusted to take care of everything you need. Every other man or woman who has committed his or her life to Jesus Christ has a special relationship with you—the Bible calls it being "brothers and sisters in the Lord." As in any other family, its members do not always see eye to eye about things, and they may have totally different personalities and abilities. Nevertheless, whether they come from London or Tokyo, Boston or Nairobi, Christians have one all-important thing in common. They have all come into the family in the same way—through trusting Jesus Christ as their Saviour.

Not only are you a newborn in a worldwide family, but you yourself are a new person. The Bible says so. "If any one is in Christ, he is a new creation; the old has passed away, behold, the new has come" (2 Cor. 5:17).

Now this is a statement of fact, and is true, whether you feel it is or not. People's reactions to becoming a Christian vary tremendously. Some individuals really feel "new all over," and know immediately and with absolute certainty that their life has done a complete about-face. Others feel no different at first, and can easily wonder if anything really happened to them at all. If they rely upon feelings. But to rely on one's emotions is unnecessary and can be dangerous. Does this mean that feelings do not count at all? Of course not. God has given us our emotions and He wants us to sense His love and friendship. This is one of the reasons why Jesus Christ gives every new Christian His gift of the Holy Spirit to live within his or her very personality. He reassures us that we are really God's children. The Bible says, "The Spirit Himself bears witness with our spirit that we are children of God" (Rom. 8:16).

However, feelings should not be the foundation of your faith. As we all know, feelings can vary from day to day according to the behavior of our friends and family and the state of our hormones—to mention just a few factors! So how can you know that you are a Christian; that the past is forgiven and forgotten, and that Jesus Christ is always with you, moment by moment through the most humdrum day? You can know it because God says so in the Bible. Trust His promises; unlike your feelings, they do not change.

On the days when you are "not sure" of your new relationship with God, make use of these verses from the Bible: "For God so loved the world (which includes you) that He gave His only begotten Son, that whoever believes in Him should not perish, but have eternal life" (John 3:16); "Behold, I stand at the door and knock; if anyone hears My voice and opens the door, I will come in to him" (Rev. 3:20).

God loves you. If you have believed and opened the door of your life to Jesus, then you are a Christian and you have God's gift of eternal life.

Many verses from the Bible assure us that God will forgive our sins. Here are two from the Old Testament: "He has not dealt with us according to our sins, or rewarded us according to our iniquities. As far as the east is from the west, so far has He removed our transgressions from us" (Ps. 103:10, 12).

With the mistakes of the past put far behind you, you can enjoy the company of Jesus Christ every day. It does not matter that you cannot see Him or hear Him speaking audibly; you have His promise, "Lo, I am with you always, to the end of the age" (Matt. 28:20).

So much for knowing that you are a new person safely within the Christian family. What happens next? Well, you start to grow up! Just as a baby needs the right sort of food to enable him to grow, so a new Christian needs the food that God has given in the Bible. Neglect the Bible and you will stay a baby Christian all your life.

### Where Do You Start?

You have taken the family Bible down off the

shelf and blown the dust off its covers or you've just rushed home with a brand-new copy. Now what do you do? One thing that you do *not* do is to start at the beginning of Genesis and aim to plod right through to the end of Revelation. The Bible is not just one book; it is a complete library of 66 books within one cover. Just like you do not give a newborn meat and potatoes for dinner, so you as a new Christian needs to start with "the milk of the word." There will be plenty of time to tackle the difficult books when you have cut some spiritual teeth.

But before we consider which parts of the Bible to read, let's think of which version of the Bible you should read them from. If you have a Bible at all, it is probably the King James Version, well-known, trusted and loved, but sometimes hard to understand. There are so many paraphrases and recent translations available that there is no need to be stuck with something that you cannot understand. The New American Standard Bible is similar enough to the King James Version for you to feel at home, and yet is more modern and understandable. Two contemporary versions are the New Testament in Modern English (Phillips) which puts the New Testament into everyday English, and the Living Bible which makes the whole Bible read like a novel. Use one of these side by side with your KJV and let each throw light on the other.

## What Do You Read?

Start with the Gospel of John, which teaches so much about Jesus Himself, and what He offers to and expects of His followers. When you have read

John's Gospel, you may want to follow a systematic program of reading a certain number of chapters each day—three chapters on weekdays and five on Sundays will take you through the Bible in one year.

But whatever method you use, and whichever part of the Bible you begin with, start off by asking God to speak to you as you read. Then read the verses slowly and carefully. Ask yourself some of these questions as you go along and write down the answers in a notebook if you wish.

1. Do I understand what the writer is talking about? (If the answer is no, try reading the same verses in another version.)
2. What does this passage teach me about God the Father, the Son, and the Holy Spirit?
3. What does it teach me about life? Is there a warning to note, a good example to follow, a promise, or a command to obey?
4. Is there a verse, or part of a verse, which has something special to say to me that I can remember and think and pray about during the day?

Mary likes to read her Bible in the following way. First, she reads straight through the verses that she has chosen for that day. Then she goes back and looks at one or two verses at a time, asking herself the questions. As the Holy Spirit brings points to her attention she stops and prays about them before going any further. In this way, God speaks to her and then she answers. For instance, when she read in the Gospel of Mark about Jesus getting up very early to pray, she realized that He had set an example for her to follow. Right away she prayed for help to get up before the rest of the family to talk to God—and then she set her alarm to go off earlier the next morning! Listen to God speaking to you, answer Him and then do what He says. Following a properly balanced Scriptural diet will help you grow as a Christian.

## Prayer Is Talking to God

There is more to prayer than talking to God about what you have just read in the Bible, even though this is important. And this is where many people get stuck. Thousands of books have been written on the subject of prayer, and as we live we will learn more and more of what it means to really communicate with God. This simple truth will always remain the same: Prayer is talking to God anywhere, at any time, about anything.

Prayer is conversing *with* God. If you have been brought up in a church where prayers are read out of a book, where the congregation mumbled the Lord's prayer mechanically, then the idea of talking to God on your own may seem strange. But take a deep breath, think of God as your loving Father who's ready to listen, and give it a try. God knows you through and through; every fault, every good point, every thought. He loves you just as you are, so there is no need to put on an act. God is the one person in the whole world with whom you can be completely open. So talk to Him—about everything. If you still feel that you need some guidelines, then try praying the book of the Bible, like this:

A—Adoration: praising and worshiping God for who He is and what He has done. Reading a psalm or a hymn can sometimes help you put your thoughts into words.

C—Confession: thinking about God's holiness

will help you realize your shortcomings and confess them to God.

T—Thanksgiving: for forgiveness and every good gift that God showers on you.

S—Supplication; praying for the needs of others as well as yourself.

You can talk to God just where you are. You do not have to be in a church building to pray; and it is not essential to close your eyes or kneel down. There are times when you may do all of these things. But you can also pray while you are washing the dishes, polishing the floor or driving the car—and at these times it is probably best to keep your eyes open!

You can talk to God at any time of the day or night—He is always listening. Most Christians like to talk over the coming day with God as soon as possible after they wake up, but it would be sad to limit the conversation only to the morning. You can ask for help with a problem, admit that you have done something wrong and ask for forgiveness, and pray for the needs of friends and family just as the need arises. This is what the apostle Paul meant when he said, "Pray without ceasing" (1 Thes. 5:17). We cannot spend all our time on our knees, but we can be in constant touch with headquarters. No detail is too small for God to bother with; no problem too huge to bring to Him without complete confidence.

But perhaps you are thinking that Bible reading and praying all sounds good, but how am I even going to find time for it? If you feel like this don't worry—you are not alone. Finding time to be alone to pray and read the Bible is always difficult. Yet it is essential if you are to grow as a Christian.

Stop and think. What time is best for you? Early in the day is ideal, before the rush really gets under way. Then you can bring all the day's details to God, ask for help where you know you will need it, and hear God speaking to you as you read the Bible. But maybe you feel that the early buzz of your alarm will turn your family against you. Well, God can waken you without an alarm if you ask Him to! Or if you are the type who is not fully awake until after breakfast, then pick up your Bible as soon as the family is out the door. Pre-schoolers and even toddlers can learn to be reasonably quiet while you "talk to Jesus." Don't give up too easily and settle for an evening post-mortem with God. Work hard to find those few minutes early in the day to get in touch with Jesus. You will find it much easirer to spend the rest of the day in harmony with Him.

# 3

# Sharing

# the Good News

Good news just asks to be shared! When you realize what the good news of the Christian faith is all about, it's natural to want to rush off to tell your family and friends what they are missing! You long for them to share your joy and peace. You want to discover God's purpose, not just for yourself as an individual, but for the whole family.

Maybe your husband and older children have shared your search for a purpose in life. If so, they will be delighted to hear about your new-found faith and will want to explore it with you. But do not be too disappointed if the reaction of your family is very different. The Bible tells us that people who are not Christians are blind to the truth about God, until God Himself opens their eyes (2 Cor.4:4-6). Remember too that a sense of need is essential before anyone can accept what God has to offer, and the journey to the point of admitting that need is often long and slow.

Perhaps those closest to you think that "a little bit of religion is fine for Mom if it keeps her happy" but they don't want to know about God for themselves. Maybe they are downright skeptical about the very existence of God and would label themselves "humanist," "atheist," "agnostic," or simply "not interested." Whatever their reaction is, don't be discouraged. We are told in the Bible to be witnesses for Jesus. A witness is someone who has first-hand experience to share. There are other ways of obeying that commandment than standing in the middle of the kitchen floor preaching a sermon. Let's think of some of them.

## There's a Time to Speak

Christine became a Christian after three long years of searching, doubt, and indecision. She had heard about what Jesus Christ had to offer, had been to church on and off, and was impressed by the "extra something" that she sensed in the lives of some of the other young wives that she had met there. But although she longed to share their faith, she hung back for one very good reason—her husband, a capable scientist, was openly scornful of anything that had to do with the Christian faith.

So on the night that she decided to accept what Jesus offered, whatever the cost, Christine went home with very mixed feelings. Should she tell her husband or not? Thinking about all their discussions on the subject, she finally decided that she must tell Stuart about the step that she had taken, and braced herself for the explosion that she expected to follow. It didn't come. Stuart listened to her faltering explanation without interrupting, and then lowered his newspaper long enough to say calmly, "Well, if that's what you want, try it. We'll know soon enough if it really changes anything." Nothing more was said, but from then on, Christine's life would either prove or disprove the reality of the Christian formula to him.

## And a Time to Keep Silent

Mary thought that being a Christian meant going to church—so she excelled at church-going. She did all the right things, and went to lots of services, but that is where it ended. There was no inward change in her life, and her family was not at all impressed with her version of Christianity. Then one day she went to hear a missionary talk about his work in India, and heard how she could make a fresh start with Jesus Christ. Hardly daring to believe it, Mary took the first step of handing her life over to Jesus, and asked Him to do for her what the church services alone could not do—make her different. Of course she wanted to tell her husband that she had found the real thing at last, but she had preached at Don once too often in the past. So Mary felt that she must go home, say nothing, and live a new life, in this way proving to herself and her family that something had really happened.

For Mary actions came first while Christine had to prove the truth of what she said by what she did. Either can be true for a new Christian. Home circumstances and reactions vary widely but no matter how you try to explain your commitment to Jesus with words, your actions will prove that your new faith is real and will make the deepest impression on those who know you best. If actions speak louder than words, how can you start to share Jesus with the family through what you do?

First of all, ask the Lord to show you where changes are needed in practical areas, then concentrate on one thing at a time.

Mary was married to a farmer who got up way before dawn to see about the animals. Never once in their married life had Mary cooked his breakfast—in fact he cooked hers. So the first step in Mary's "no speaking—all action" campaign was simple—she got up and cooked Don's breakfast. Not just once, but every day. And that was just the beginning of the revolution that Jesus brought about in her everyday life. Little by little He showed her where she was falling short in the ordinary practical things of life, and little by little enabled her to make changes. Since she had been a "don't-carish" home-maker in the past, Don could not help but see the difference.

Perhaps you have always been a model housewife, and don't need to change in this particular way. Still, in every marriage there are friction points where a change in your attitude would really show. Just one word of warning. Make sure that the change you are making is one that brings pleasure to the other person, and not just to yourself. Let's see how this works out.

The lawn was the thing that came between Sally and Steve. To Sally, yardwork was a man's job—her father had always done everything outside their home. In Steve's childhood the garden had been as much a part of his mother's domain as the house—and he did not expect to do more than mow the lawn occasionally. When Sally became a Christian she decided to share Jesus with her husband by making their home even more comfortable and attractive—a job that she loved. She went to flower arranging classes and took up patchwork quilting. She enjoyed it and made lots of new friends.

She was hurt when this way of witnessing to Steve didn't make much of an impression on him. Of course, the flower arrangements made him sneeze and his favorite battered sports shirt had been sacrificed for a patchwork quilt so it was not surprising. It took Sally a while to see that she was on the wrong track. Then the truth dawned. The change in her that the Lord wanted to see lay outside the house and in her private battleground, the yard. It was quite a struggle for a day or two, but when at last with a shrug and a smile Sally put away the quilt and went out and bought a pair of gardening gloves, Steve did not need to be told that something real had happened in her life.

With Jenny it was not quilting, it was baking. She loved cooking and making cakes was her speciality. When she wanted to make up to her husband for a difference in opinion, or show him what a good Christian wife she was, she would bake him a cake. It was always a blue-ribbon cake, but the only trouble was Paul did not like cake very much. He would have preferred that she had made love to him.

Don't be shocked. Jesus can even be shared in this most intimate part of marriage. The physical relationship can be the source of tremendous joy or considerable friction. Instead of telling a wife to leave her husband, or move into another bedroom when she becomes a Christian, Paul said quite clearly that "if a Christian woman has a husband who isn't a Christian, and he wants her to stay with him, she must not leave him" (1 Cor. 7:13, LB). But more than that, he said earlier, "The man should give his wife all that is her right as a married woman, and the wife should do the same for her husband" (v. 3). This means being the very best wife in every sense of the word. Perhaps you need to ask His help in making a good relationship even better. Maybe you have a "mini" marriage—with you making the *minimum* response to his *minimum* requirements, and making excuses the rest of the time. If so, be glad that Jesus can help you change here too, for this can be a very powerful witness.

## When to Speak

Actions may speak louder than words but there will be a time and a place for words too. When comments are made about the changes in your life don't be afraid to explain why, and give Jesus the credit. Resist the temptation to preach or argue about church or religion. You may have to agree to disagree about theology but you can talk with confidence about what Jesus has done for you. If your actions are consistent with your words, no one can disprove you!

So far we have thought about being witnesses for Jesus to your immediate family and friends. But what about those outside your family circle? Should you hurriedly offer your services to your understaffed Sunday School, the youth group, or the women's Bible study group? It is very easy to feel that you are only doing something that counts for Jesus, if that something takes place outside your own home. If the family seems disinterested or is unresponsive to your efforts to show them what it means to be a Christian, then it seems much more rewarding for you to concentrate your efforts somewhere else.

Think and pray carefully, however, before you take on regular Christian activities that will take you out of your home a great deal. If God has given you a home and a family, then you have the first responsibility to take Jesus to your family. If you are a new Christian you will have a lot to learn before you can teach other people. This does not mean that you have to be a theologian before you can witness for Jesus, but it is important to know what you believe and why. Of course Sunday School teachers and youth workers are needed, and maybe you will be asked to serve God in this way later on. But in the meantime, do not overlook the chances you have now to do small things for others. Shopping for an elderly neighbor, looking after a toddler while his mother goes downtown, being available to drive the school bus when the driver's baby is ill, can all be done as a service for the Lord, and can give opportunities to spread the Good News in deed as well as in word. Each day you will have new opportunities—reach out with open arms and take the ones He gives.

So much for words and actions in sharing the Good News. The other side of the coin is even more important.

## Speaking to God

"Sometimes talk to those around you about God. Always talk to God about those around you." This essential part of being a witness for Jesus can never be overdone. Unless we are in touch with headquarters ourselves, we can work and talk until we are exhausted, and it will have no effect at all. But when we pray, God can work through us.

Maybe you are saying, "If this is true, why have I been praying for ages for my husband to become a Christian and nothing seems to happen?" Well, there is more involved in prayer than just begging God to reveal Himself to those we love. What about your motives—why are you praying so earnestly for your husband, child, or friend? Is it because you feel your life would be easier, or your happiness more complete if your loved ones shared your faith? Be honest! Or is it because you want them to know the joy of life with Jesus and to be able to face death without fear? Of course any of these desires will prompt you to pray, and rightfully so. But what about God's part in all this? He is the One who has gone to such lengths to make it possible for people to come back to Him, and your first motive for praying should be for His glory. Then we should pray for the sake of the person concerned. You come into it last of all! When God helps you see this and enables you to pray with true unselfishness, you will begin to see your prayers answered positively.

So pray for guidance in how you act. Pray for wisdom in what you say and what you do not. And pray for the Holy Spirit to open the eyes of your loved ones to their needs and His resources. Always remember that God is not depending on you to make anyone a Christian. You have a part to play, but you cannot do the Holy Spirit's work for Him. So, being a witness for Jesus is, as someone has put it, "Sharing Jesus, in the power of the Holy Spirit, and leaving the results to God." And this you can do with absolute confidence.

# 4

# The Children

"I was so excited about Jesus that I had to tell someone about Him, so I talked to Chris." Barbara was talking about her early days as a Christian to her friends in their weekly Bible study group. "He hadn't started school yet and we were home together all day. It was tremendous to see his faith flicker into life and grow."

"Are you suggesting that a child that young have a personal faith? Surely it's just that anything you say is right to them just because you have said it?" Christine, the scientist's wife, sounded a little dubious.

"Yes, I do believe that the Holy Spirit can help even a small child to have a personal faith—Chris certainly had one and still has. But I agree that mothers have a tremendous influence on children up to junior high age, which needs to be very carefully used. There's the danger of them saying that they believe, just to please you, if they know that's the answer you want. And that's useless. It's got to come from the child himself."

"There's no danger of that with my two brats," said Jane plaintively. "It's almost impossible to get them to church without a fight. They know that their father rarely goes to church, and besides, no ten- or twelve-year-old wants to sit for more than two minutes at a time, so they don't want to come with me."

"I think that lots of boys—and girls too for that matter—go through a phase at that age." Elizabeth was the oldest member of the group and the mother of several teenagers. "It happens in homes where both parents are Christians, as well as those where they are not. My children were well into their teens before even I became a Christian, so I couldn't delude myself into thinking I could force them to go to church. But when they noticed changes in me, they were curious and started coming along sometimes to find out what was going on."

"Yes, I think that's the way to deal with older children," said Sally, joining the conversation rather shyly. "I was getting into a terrible stew the other night because Steve was a couple of hours late getting home, and hadn't called or anything. Penny said to me, 'Mommy, I thought Christians weren't supposed to worry.' It made me stop and think, especially since we've never really talked about me being a Christian before."

"Well, I don't think I have changed very much—or not so my family would notice," said Jane sadly. "What do you do if they don't seem to want to know. I mean, it's bad enough having to worry how they're doing in school, who their friends are, and how much freedom to give them without this as well. And it really underlies all the rest doesn't it? How do you teach children about Christian things in our materialistic society, and get it across to them that it's real—the only reality, in fact, in spite of what they might hear from other people?"

## Answering Questions

Well, how do you? How do you start to share the reality and excitement of living day by day with Jesus, with the children in your family who may vary in age from toddlers to teenagers?

If, like Barbara, you are at home all day with pre-schoolers, you will have plenty of opportunities to talk to them quite naturally about Jesus, answering the questions they ask from morning to night. (You know what I mean!)

"Why are you reading that book, Mommy?"

"This is God's special book; it's called the Bible and tells us all about Him."

"Who's God?"—a natural lead-in to explain God in terms of His creation; something even a small child can begin to grasp.

"Why have you got your eyes shut, Mommy? Wake up!" (Prod, prod!)

"I'm talking to God, and asking Him to help me with all my jobs today. In a minute we'll talk to Him together."

If you have your own Bible reading and prayer time after breakfast, or at some other time when the children are around, this can be a good time to give them a Bible story book to look at. A Bible story and group prayer can follow your own prayer time. If time is short, after lunch might be a good time to tell or read a Bible story. The important thing is that Jesus should be an integral part of your everyday life.

Of course, questions will not be reserved only for times like these. Small children ask the most unexpected things at times, and take our replies literally. When our second son was about a year old, I was sorting out some baby clothes to pack away. Our almost three-year-old son was helping and soon wanted to know what I was going to do with all these things. I explained that we would put some of the things away, in case we had another baby to wear them, and give the rest away to little babies who had nothing to wear.

"Are we going to have another baby?" he wanted to know. This was a good question since my husband and I were still praying about it.

"Daddy and I will have to ask the Lord Jesus whether He wants us to have any more children," I answered slowly.

"Well, I want to ask Him now," said David firmly. Somewhat taken aback I prayed a short prayer asking that Jesus would show us whether He wanted us to have another baby or not. Then he opened his eyes and gazed at me expectantly.

"Did He say yes or no?"

Questions come and go, and get more complicated as children grow older. It is a good principle to keep answers simple and to the point, without giving more information than is being asked for at that time. Some questions have to be answered many times before the answer is really grasped, but in an effort to be simple, never say something that you will have to take back later.

Of course, there are many questions that have no simple, complete answers, and it is never wrong to admit that you do not know. If the answer can be found, then look for it together; if it is one of life's imponderables, then say so, assuring them at the same time that God is all-knowing and can safely be left to take care of these things.

What happens if the school teaches one thing and you teach another? In a sense this clash of views has to come sometime, and every child has to face it. It is often helpful if your children can talk over these problems with a Christian adult other than yourself, so that they can see that other people believe these things as well as you. In addition, there are many helpful Christian books on such subjects as evolution and the evidence for the resurrection. Read and discuss them together, and then stand aside, prayerfully leaving the Holy Spirit to do the job of conviction that only He can do.

Look on questions as an opportunity, not a threat, and do not be embarrassed if these questions come up when other adults are present. Sue's husband realized that his idea of what the Christian faith was all about was quite different from hers simply by hearing her answer the children's questions. It was at this point that his own search for God began.

It is a very difficult calling to be a Christian mother in today's world when materialistic and other anti-Christian pressures bombard our children from every side. In what ways should our Christian standards influence the way we run our homes? Can these standards be set down for young people who may not understand or agree with them? Well, all products operate best when used according to the manufacturer's instructions, and this applies as well to children. The Bible says a lot about family life, but we will focus on three basic needs that God instilled in everyone, including children. They are things that every Christian mother can try, with God's help, to provide.

## A Sense of Identity

Everyone needs to be a person in his or her own right. God recognized this in His dealings with people in Bible times, and met with them as individuals, calling each by name. This sense of being an individual, a person who counts, is terribly important to all of us. Teach your children that they each have a special part of God's love; that He knows them by name and has a plan for each individual life. And if you have more than one child, try to avoid lumping them all together. You know what I mean: saying "the children," "the boys," or "the twins" instead of "John and Andrew."

When bedtime comes, try to spend a few minutes with each child, talking with him or her, listening to the day's adventures, and, if he is old enough to enjoy it, helping him read his Bible and pray. Several publishers produce Bible story books for children from four years old and up since it is at this age that queries and problems about the Christian faith can be brought into the open. Resist the temptation to be with more than one child at a time. You will be tempted if they share a bedroom, or you are tired and looking forward to some peace and quiet. Apart from the fact that two is company and three is a crowd when it comes to sharing secrets, the problems of one child can easily confuse another. A first-grader needs things explained differently than his fourth-grade brother.

When it comes to praying, pause for a moment and ask the Lord for a sense of His reality and nearness. Avoid the blanket "Bless everyone in the world. Amen" approach. Even here the individual touch comes in. "God bless Grandma" is a good start—but what particular blessing does she need? Not just "God bless Daddy" but "Help Daddy with that special job he has to do."

## The Need to Be Accepted

"You're out!"

"No, I'm not!"

"Yes, you are."

Our children hate to be told that—do yours? We all need to be accepted by those around us, and many of us, children included, spend anxious hours trying to be what we're not in order to be acceptable in our particular group.

One of the most relaxing things about being a Christian is knowing that God accepts us as we are, not as we ought to be. Can this knowledge enable you to accept your children for what they are? Can you encourage them to develop their own God-given potential to the fullest? God intends us to. We may have to face up to the fact that Mary will never be a nurse, but will probably find her niche in life as a computer programmer; that Steve will never go to a university, but has all the makings of an excellent mechanic. Can your children, especially the older ones, hold views different from yours about politics, about their future plans, and, most difficult of all, about Christianity, without getting the feeling that you would love them much more if they thought like you?

God's love is never conditional. We need to pray for His kind of love, again and again. Children should be able to express their doubts and ask questions without any fear of being less acceptable to you. Above all avoid the unspoken division between those who are Christians in your family and those who are not—like Mommy's side and Daddy's side—with one group consciously or unconsciously looking down on the other. Always remember that any Christian who tries to share his or her faith is only one beggar telling another beggar where to find bread.

Having told them, we must prayerfully stand back and allow each of them to make his or her own choice about whether to go and find it. It's hard, but it's the only way. A family that can acknowledge the importance of each individual, and can give everyone the right to be themselves, accepted and loved for what they are, will certainly have their share of lively discussion. They may lack the superficial peacefulness of those who insist on an outward conformity to one way of thinking and living. But it is an atmosphere in which God can work, because this is His way with people.

## Absolute Freedom within Limits

While children should be accepted as the individuals that they are, this does not mean that they should be allowed to do exactly as they please. Family life would be unbearable if every member did his own thing with total disregard for the needs and convenience of others. Children need to be trained to be considerate, helpful, responsible, and obedient. In setting limits for acceptable behavior, we are following the pattern of God's dealings with mankind from the beginning of time. In the very first chapters of the Bible we read how God gave men and women complete authority over their surroundings, with one exception. When this condition was broken, inevitable consequences followed. (You can read about it in Genesis 3.)

Together parents need to agree on the boundaries of behavior that are appropriate for the ages and stages of their children, and make sure that the children understand what is expected of them, as well as the reasons for the limits and the penalty for disobedience. If only one parent is, as yet, a fully committed Christian, then you may not be able to arrive at limits which you would consider ideal, but having decided on a workable arrangement (preceded by a lot of prayer) stick to it and back each other up at all times. Children need the security of united parents and though they may rebel against the rules laid down for them, the rules form a welcome safety barrier behind which to retreat when the pressures of their peer-group friends get too hot to handle.

## Prayer

And so we come to our main weapon—prayer. In our own strength, we can do our best to order our family life according to God's principles and perhaps produce a reasonably happy and well-balanced home. But if we are to help our children find their places in God's plan, knowing that they are accepted by Him, and experiencing the security and peace of living within the framework of His laws, we must fuel the whole operation with prayer.

First we must pray that God will work in our own lives, so that we can be, in His strength, the sort of mother He can use. Then, every day we must bring every problem to Him for His guidance and help. Things may not work out according to your plan. Life probably won't go smoothly—the Holy Spirit has a habit of turning our preconceived notions upside down. But if we live life this way, we can say with Paul, "We know that God causes all things to work together for good to those who love God" (Rom. 8:28). Do we need any greater assurance for the well-being of our families than that?

# 5

# The Day that
# Is Different

"Sunday? It's the busiest day in the week! Everyone in our family wants to do something different, and I seem to spend all day making sandwiches and getting meals at odd times—once I've gotten them out of bed!"

"Sunday? I would like to spend it just thinking about God—with absolute quietness to worship and read . . . but of course, the family . . ."

"Sunday was a dull day when I was a kid. 'Don't do this, don't do that' . . . I don't want my children to hate it like I did, so it's almost like any other day for us."

"Being a working wife, I have to spend the weekend catching up with the chores, but I do try to go to church once a week. I think that is all God expects."

Four very different views of the first day of the week—as different as the personalities and circumstances of the women who expressed them. What sort of day is Sunday to you? Perhaps it was just the second day of the weekend before you became a committed Christian, but now you are wondering whether there should be any difference in this area of your life. Maybe you feel that keeping Sunday special with all kinds of restrictions went out with the Victorians and you are glad it did—and yet you have the uneasy feeling that the week would go by much easier if in the rush of everyday living some time were set aside for God.

Whatever our personal opinions may be, there is no doubt that the Bible teaches that one day in seven should be different. In fact, it was so important in God's scheme of things that it was included in the ten foundational laws for the Israelites' national life that we know as the Ten Commandments.

## A Day to Remember

When Moses passed on God's laws to the Israelites for the first time, he told them that the Sabbath (their equivalent of our Sunday) was to be set apart for God, so that they could worship Him, and remember how He had set them free from Egyptian slavery.

They had a great deliverance to celebrate, but Christians have a far greater one as they think each Sunday of the resurrection of Jesus and the way back to God that He has made for them. Sunday is our day to remember, and for most of us this involves going to church.

## Is It Necessary to Go to Church?

Going to church does not make you a Christian, but once you are a Christian you need the family of

Christians who meet to worship in a local group, and they need you. The Bible speaks quite plainly about this. "Let us not neglect our church meetings, as some people do, but encourage and warn each other, especially now that the day of His coming back again is drawing near" (Heb. 10:25, LB).

For a few Christian women, worshiping in church on Sunday (or, even more rarely, at all) is impossible because their husbands forbid them. But for most of us whose husbands do not accompany us, church-going is possible if we make the effort to go. At best, we may be cheerfully waved off, or at worst our going is tolerated as long as they do not have to be involved. Church-going is possible if we are willing to make the effort.

## Which Church?

There is no such thing as a perfect church! How could there be when every church is made up of many different people, each with his own hopes and fears, strengths and weaknesses. But there is at least one particular group of Christians, working and worshiping together in your locality among whom God has a place for you. Your job is to find out who they are.

This is not always easy. You may be naturally inclined toward the close informality of a small mission hall, or the soaring beauty of a liturgical service in a great cathedral—or anything in between. Setting aside your personal preference, you know that you need to belong somewhere where others know and love Jesus as the living Saviour and Lord. To help you grow as a Christian you need to hear the Bible taught and explained as the inspired word of God that it is. Ideally your church should be nearby, so that you are worshiping and sharing Jesus with those among whom you live and work. There are many factors to consider before you find your best alternative. Be prepared for some surprises; God's people rarely are ideal!

What guidelines do you follow as you decide to join one particular church?

*Pray.* Talk to God about it. Ask Him to show you His choice, and to help you to accept it willingly.

*Look first at the familiar.* If you were already a fairly regular worshipper at one particular church before you became a committed Christian, stay where you are, unless or till God shows you that you should move.

Sally was in this position. Some of her Christian friends pressed her to leave the staid traditional church in which she had worshiped for several years. In many ways she would have liked to, but having prayed about it, she just did not feel that this was the right thing to do. Sally was aware that she needed more help in understanding the Bible than she was getting from the Sunday services, so she asked a Christian friend to meet her for Bible study once a week. The group soon grew from two to a dozen, some of them from Sally's church. For many of these women, hearing the Bible explained in practical terms was something new and exciting; through them God started to work in a new way in this church.

Jane's experience was different. She had worshipped at Sally's church for a long while, but when she became a Christian—through what she had heard at the Bible study group—God led her to a church of a different denomination for two or three years. There she learned much about the Bible and the Christian life, and really grew as a Christian. But God did not leave her there. Having equipped her, He showed her through circumstances that she must go back to her original church, and help Sally share the reality of their faith with others in that particular congregation.

*Sum up the strange.* If you have no ties with any church, talk to Christian friends, and visit their churches a few times until you get the inner assurance that this is God's place for you. If you've moved since you became a Christian, look for a church that meets together during the week for Bible study and prayer. Above all be prepared to give as well as to receive—God can and will work miracles in a fellowship where there are even two or three who are prepared to pray and find out His will, and then do it.

## Who Goes and How Often?

Ideally the whole family should worship together at least one of the Sunday services. Is this ideal completely removed from your reality? Don't despair. Keep the ideal in mind and work towards it, but be prepared to be adaptable, like Barbara.

"Church! Church! Church! That's all I seem to hear about these days!" Sam was letting his feelings be known in no uncertain terms! "I like our Sundays as they are, and so did you until a few months ago. I'm not giving up my jogging on Sunday morning just so that you can go and waste your time in that church. If you want to go, you'll have to take the kids with you, and that's that."

As you can see, Barbara had a real problem. The church she attended had a nursery for babies, that was all, and the service did not meet the needs of elementary children. Sunday School was too early and the evening service was out of the question—Sunday dinner with his mother was something else Sam was not ready to give up. Barbara found a solution to her problem as she prayed about it with a Christian friend. She introduced Barbara to a church where the Sunday morning service was a family service in which the whispers and the thuds of dropped hymn books went unnoticed. Sunday School for the children during the sermon provided teaching that they could understand. From then on church going for Barbara and the children was much less frustrating. Others may have to make different concessions for the sake of maintaining family harmony.

Like Sam, Diana's husband is not very sympathetic to her attending church and says he will never go himself. At the moment Diana keeps the peace by getting up for the early morning service, so that his day is not interfered with, while the children go to Sunday School. For Janet, attending church on Sunday means doing the extra Saturday preparation necessary to enable the whole family to drive ten miles to church—because this is the one church to which Tim will consent to go. Since Mike insists on eating Sunday lunch at 12:30 sharp, Sue goes to church on Sunday evening. Be adaptable, but be there—if it is humanly possible.

Of course you will want to do everything in your power to encourage the rest of your family to be there with you. Younger children will probably like to come with you to a short service or to Sunday School. Husbands and teenagers respond better to a smiling casual invitation than a long face and nagging! Be open to the possibility that an invitation (by someone else!) to a church youth group, an after-church party and discussion may be more appealing to your teenagers than the Sunday morning service. Remember above all that nothing is gained and a lot is lost if the matter of church attendance becomes a battleground. So if you have to go alone for a while, go cheerfully and ask God to make such a difference in your life and behavior that the rest of the family will be drawn, in spite of themselves, to discover the reason why.

## A Day to Rest

Few busy wives and mothers would argue about the need for a day of rest. Fortunately, this is part of God's plan for all His creatures. Moses was quite specific about it. Every one of the Israelites, from the head of the house down to the humblest employee, was to have one day in seven free from his regular work.

And yet while acknowledging the need for a change of pace, few of us take any practical steps to obey the command. "A woman's work is never done," we quote glibly, and then wonder why, having ignored the Maker's instructions, we do not function or cope with life as well as we could.

Is it possible to make Sunday a "day of rest" when you have a husband and family depending on you? Yes, it is possible, but it is not easy, and it requires determination and discipline to achieve. It is very easy to start off with a rush of enthusiasm, keep on top of the housework, and do extra preparation on Saturday so that Sunday can be a rest day for a couple of weeks. Then comes a Saturday when you are extra busy, so you leave just a few jobs "until tomorrow" and your good intentions go down the drain.

So first of all engrave this principle on your heart: On Sundays I will keep routine chores to a minimum because this is something that God has ordered for my good, and it is a command for me to obey. Now obviously the things that constitute "routine chores" will vary from household to household. A mother with a baby and young children will have more to do than one with older teenagers. We must avoid copying the example of the religious leaders in Jesus' time (and others like them since) who made the do's and don'ts for Sunday such a burden that the spirit behind it was completely lost.

You don't have to think that the rest of the family will suffer from neglect or miss their special dinner. Vegetables can be cooked ahead on Saturday, and coffeecake or desserts made. A quick once-over with a dustcloth and a vacuum will cut out the need for any real housework, and if you see something that needs attention on Sunday, ignore it with a clear conscience—it's your day off!

The family may find this new policy a little strange at first, but even if they cannot appreciate the spiritual reasons behind it, most of them will agree that mother has a right to one day off a week. (Especially when they reap the benefits of having someone who is better able to cope with the stress and strains of the other six days.)

## A Day to Rejoice
God intends us to be happy and enjoy this day which is His gift for our well-being, and yet this element of rejoicing often seems to be missing as

we rest and remember God on His day. How can we make this day enjoyably different for everyone in the family?

In this our attitude is all-important. If our hearts are peaceful because we are not worrying about weekday problems, and full of gladness because Jesus is alive, then the whole atmosphere of the home will be affected. What we do with the hours we do not spend in worship will vary considerably from family to family. In those homes where the majority are committed Christians, activities will be quite different from those in homes where only one person loves the Lord Jesus. But whatever our circumstances, we can follow the example of Jesus as He worshiped, spent time with His disciples, prayed for them often, and was always ready to help those in need.

Enjoyment of God's good gifts often starts at a very practical level. How about letting everyone choose a favorite food for a meal. Freshly brewed coffee for breakfast, cola for lunch, or a special dessert can make Sunday special in our house. (Doing something special doesn't necessarily mean more work for you.) Your family might prefer a picnic on the patio to an inside meal on a summer Sunday; hearty soup and sandwiches in the kitchen are more fun after a wintry afternoon at the zoo.

## A Day to Communicate

"We just don't have time to talk anymore; someone's always dashing off somewhere; we're all too busy." If your house is more like Grand Central Station than a peaceful oasis from Monday to Saturday, then use Sunday to get to know each other a little better. It is no use complaining that your teenagers use the house like a hotel and never confide in you if you have been too busy to forge the links of communication when they were younger.

In our house, Sunday is Family Day. Our children are not allowed to disappear out the door to roam all day with friends—a major restriction. To compensate, each member of the family takes turns choosing what we do on Sunday afternoon and the rest must go along with the choice without grumbling. In this way we may spend one Sunday feeding the ducks at the park, another playing catch in the yard and a third asking the next-door neighbors in for games—but whatever is done, everyone joins in.

## A Day to Share

"I want to give and give until it hurts," sighed Kate. "I want to share our home on Sunday with people who can't pay us back—old people, students, even transients—but Jim can't see further than his own family circle, so it's Sunday dinner with relatives nearly every week!"

This situation causes tension in many families. One member wants to use Sunday to share with everyone the good things that God has given; another feels family and close friends come first and others run a very poor second. What can you do if this is your problem?

Again the solution requires flexibility. It may be possible to occasionally invite the lonely and the needy to share your home on Sundays—but be equally willing to welcome relatives who, though they may seem to have everything, need Jesus just as much as the others. However unsympathetic they may seem, you may be the only Christian they know—the only one who can demonstrate His love in action.

If you cannot invite people to your home, maybe you can be like Sylvia who spends the time that the children are at Sunday School and her husband is reading the paper, with the widow up the street. Or perhaps you can give Mrs. Andrews a lift to church when you go, or write a letter to Mrs. Best in the hospital. There are so many ways of sharing God's goodness with others as a part of Sunday doing what we can with a willing heart and above all, cheerfully, remembering that "Cheerful givers are the ones God prizes" (2 Cor. 9:7, LB).

# 6

# You're Not
# the Girl I Married

"The girl that I marry will have to be soft and feminine!" That's one man's vision of his future wife; not quite in the idiom of today's teenagers, of course! Nevertheless, it is true that each of us brings to marriage a picture of the ideal husband or wife. The way this picture takes shape depends on many factors. A girl is influenced more than she realizes by what her father was like, and whether or not she had a good relationship with him. The books she read and the television and films she saw in her pre-marriage years, all combine to give her a mental picture of the kind of man who will fulfill her particular needs and complement her character. A similar process occurs with a man—he is influenced by what his mother was like.

## When He's Less Than Ideal
While we may realize before marriage that our

real-life partner-to-be has a few of the ideal characteristics missing from his make-up, we confidently think that we can make the necessary altera-
tions. What we do not realize is that our partner
may have the same plans for us, and at this point
trouble can start.

Probably you have a pretty clear idea of what you
want from your husband and your marriage. If you
have been married for any length of time those
ideas have had to be modified somewhat. But have
you ever paused to consider, or even tried to find
out what your husband wants from his marriage?
Is he basically unsure of himself, needing someone
who can support, encourage, and mother him? Perhaps he's a go-getter who expects his wife to keep
pace with him in his climb to the top and to take
all the home responsibilities off his shoulders so that
he can give his mind to outside matters. Does he
want a model housekeeper, feeling that home is
home only if you are there all day to bake cookies
and clean house—or will he cheerfully exist on convenience foods so that both of you can work?

Of course, over the years, every couple changes to
a greater or lesser degree as each is molded by circumstances and the pressures exerted by their
"other half." But when you become a committed
Christian a new factor comes into the marriage
which inevitably brings with it its own pressures
and possibilities.

Some women mistakenly believe that when they
become Christians they have to abandon all their
old friends and interests, neglect their appearance,
and spend their time saying no. Of course there will
be changes in your life, but make sure that they
are the ones prompted by Jesus and not by your

own ideas of what Christians should or should not do. Otherwise you may have to listen to your husband say, with absolute truthfulness, "You're not the girl I married, and you're dull, dull, dull!"

If you put yourself in this position you are being unfair to your husband and to God. It is God's plan that His children should be better marriage partners after becoming His children, not worse ones. We will improve if we follow God's plan for marriage, and make a real effort to understand our partner and his needs.

### Submission!

God's first requirement of us as Christian wives is submission to our husband's authority.

The phrase sticks in your throat, doesn't it, in these days of woman's lib? And yet the most ardent feminist has to admit that any team can have only one leader, and God has ordained that the leader in the marriage team is to be the husband. "But," you might argue, "this only applies when the husband is a Christian." That is not what the Bible says. "Wives, in the same way be submissive to your husbands so that, if any of them do not believe the word, they may be won over without talk by the behavior of their wives, when they see the purity and reverence of your lives" (1 Peter 3:1-2, NIV).

You may feel that you could never bring yourself to be genuinely submissive—in fact you bristle at the thought of it. This is true for many of us. But if you are really willing to obey God's command, and tell Him so, He will take care of the emotions involved, and enable you to be, in His strength, what you could never be on your own.

How far does this submission take us? All the

way, except on the rare occasion when submission to her husband would lead a wife to do something illegal or immoral.

The Bible says, "Wives, submit to your husbands as to the Lord" (Eph. 5:22, NIV).

This is the key. If you can go along with your husband's wishes without, at the same time, disobeying any of God's commands, then you must do so. Occasionally the line dividing the one from the other is a very fine one. If this happens, pray about the problem very carefully before you act, and if there is an ultimate clash of loyalties, remember that obedience to God comes first.

Submission to her husband does not make a Christian wife an inferior being and a doormat. She is still free to state her case, very lovingly, if she feels that her husband is leading the team in the wrong direction. But (and this is the hard part) if he is adamant, she must refrain from nagging and leave the final decision to him, trusting God to take care of the results. It may be better to pray than to speak on some occasions. God can overrule circumstances and influence decisions without our having to say a word—but remember that true submission is an attitude of heart and mind. It is all too possible to be outwardly submissive, with tight lips and a pained expression, and inwardly seething. This is not submission, and we cannot expect God to bless it. Perhaps this aspect of the marriage relationship can be summed up in Augustine's words:

"Woman was taken out of man, not from his head, to be above him, nor from his feet to be trampled under foot, but from his side to help him, from under his arm to be protected by him and from near his heart to be loved by him."

## Two Individuals—and Yet One

God has planned that a wife should follow her husband's lead, but it does not mean that she should be her husband's shadow.

"I'm just somebody's wife, and someone else's mother." Have you ever said that, feeling that your own personality is being denied? Well, you certainly count with God, and when you realize this and the fact that part of His overall plan in history can be fulfilled by you alone, then, perhaps for the first time, you will discover a sense of personal identity. Life takes on a new dimension as you see God begin to work out His plan for your life.

Now while all this is good, beware of becoming so caught up with your new Christian friends and activities that your home and family take second place. Imagine how you would feel if your husband suddenly became absorbed in a hobby with which you were neither able nor willing to be involved. Suddenly he wants to be out of the house several evenings a week; he has a new circle of friends with whom you do not feel at home—you cannot even understand what they are talking about most of the time. Your whole family life has to change to accommodate this new hobby and gradually you feel more and more shut out. Of course, that does not apply to your Christianity . . . or does it? Yes, God intends that you should be an individual, but in marriage He also intends that the two should be one, and though your first allegiance is to Him, on the human level your husband has the first rights on your loyalty and love.

Let's "accentuate the positive and eliminate the negative" as the song says. Work at your marriage. If you do not know already, find out what your husband longs for in a wife, and try to meet those needs. What if he does not talk about that? Stray comments can give clues; those light-hearted quizzes in women's magazines can be very revealing! Above all, the offer of God's wisdom applies in this, as in any other situation.

Welcome opportunities to meet people. Don't look on the social side of your life together or of your husband's job as something to be avoided whenever possible. There may be certain times when it is right to refuse an invitation, but remember that Jesus never cut Himself off from those who needed Him most. So, rather than running away, ask Him to help you on these occasions and you will find opportunities to share your faith in the most unlikely situations.

Barbara wanted to avoid the dinner dance given by Sam's firm, but there was no way of getting out of it. When she went to the powder room after dinner she knew why God had not given her an excuse to stay home. An acquaintance was huddled in a corner sobbing bitterly. Within a few moments the whole story of a broken marriage came tumbling out.

"Help me, Barbara; give me something to cling to . . ." And so, when she least expected it, Barbara was able to be the first link in the chain that eventually drew that woman to God.

What about the activities that used to fill your life but are no longer appealing to you? Of course you will want to cut out those things that do not honor Jesus Christ, but if this means there are fewer things that you can do together, look for other interests you can share with your husband. If lack of baby-sitters keeps you at home, then join a baby-sitting group or start one. Once you have gotten back into the habit of going out together again, whether it is to visit friends, take an evening class, or work with a local community group, it will be more likely that he will be happy to accompany you to the church supper or to a Christian friend's home for dessert.

Above al, don't be dull. Ask Jesus to fill your life with His joy so that you are a living example of one who is living the "life in all its fullness" that He came to give.

# 7

# A New Kind
# of Loving

What does *love* mean to you? It may mean one thing right now, and something quite different tomorrow, because it is a word we use to express a whole range of emotions. We speak of men murdering for the love of money and dying for love of country and friends. We may claim to love our favorite food, an agreeable job, or the area in which we live—but that is a very different emotion from that which we feel towards our husband and family. And none of these feelings correspond exactly to that attitude of complete self-giving referred to by Jesus, when He commanded His disciples to "love one another just as I have loved you" (John 15:12). His love for us is our example.

Love should be the hallmark of the Christian, not as some bubbling super-happy emotional state, but as a practical standard to govern our whole way of thinking and living. The Apostle Paul spelled out in down-to-earth language exactly what the out-working of Christian love entails:

> "Love is patient, love is kind, and is not jealous; love does not brag and is not arrogant, does not behave unbecomingly; it does not seek its own, is not provoked, does not take into account a wrong suffered, but rejoices with the truth; bears all things, believes all things, hopes all things, endures all things. Love never fails" (1 Cor. 13:4-8).

If you think this is asking the impossible you are quite right—humanly speaking! For this is God's own love which He pours out, that it might fill us and overflow as we deal with other people. But this does not happen without any action on our part. The Apostle Paul tells us to "make love your aim" (1 Cor. 14:1, LB). We can choose whether or not we will allow this love to flow; whether or not we are prepared to put aside our own rights and self-interests. God never forces anything on us; not even love.

## A Clean Channel for Love

How does this work out in practice? Imagine a pipe that carries water from point A to point B. If it is to work efficiently, it must be whole. If there are cracks or gaps in the walls of the pipe, its contents will soon seep out and the pipe will be empty. In the same way the Christian who wants to be a channel of God's love to a thirsty world must be whole-hearted about it. Too many of us want to play at being Christians—happy to accept the benefits so long as they do not cost us anything. That kind of Christian is like a leaking pipe, giving out a trickle where there should be a flowing stream.

A water pipe must also be clean. Dirt and leaves that get into the pipe clog it up, and the flow is slowed down and perhaps almost stopped. What hampers the flow of God's love in your life? Yourself? Self-interest, self-love—the attitudes that run contrary to the self-sacrificing love that Paul describes? Perhaps it is disobedience, rebellion against some aspect of God's dealings with you. Perhaps unbelief is clogging up the channel of your life. God knows what it is, and He will show you and help you deal with it if you really want Him to.

The most important thing for our water pipe is to be connected to the source of supply. This means allowing the Holy Spirit to work in our lives. The Bible tells us that love is the first fruit, or result, of the Holy Spirit's activity in our lives—but again we have to allow Him to produce it. Every Christian has the Holy Spirit in his or her life, but the Holy Spirit does not *have* every Christian. So many of us let the Holy Spirit have control over one small part of our life—but keep the rest of it very firmly in our own hands . . . just in case! This is not how God intends us to live. The Bible tells us to be filled with the Spirit (Eph. 5:18). Don't keep Him shut up in the kitchen of your life, but ask Jesus to give you His Spirit in all His fullness, so that His presence and power fills the whole house—from attic to basement! Don't be afraid of where this may lead you—love will produce love, even in the most unlovely. Only as the Holy Spirit works can we begin to put His love into practice with the one who needs and expects it most—your husband.

Marriage has a greater potential for deep happiness or utter misery than any other human relationship. Of course no one gets married intending to be unhappy; but most of us know at least one couple who started confidently together and within a few years were further apart in spirit than utter strangers. Yet if God created the marriage relationship, surely He is capable of making it work. God planned that marriage should be for the companionship, help, and comfort of the two people involved. Companionship, helping, and comforting —how much of that goes on in your home? Or is there an atmosphere of armed neutrality, with two people jealously guarding their own individual rights? Whether your marriage is reasonably happy or downright miserable, God's love can transform this relationship, if only one of the people involved will allow it to flow.

## Love in Action

Can you forgive and forget? Is your love patient and kind to your husband—with all that that involves? Are you as patient with his shortcomings as you expect him to be with yours? What about those little habits that seemed so endearing at first, but become more irritating as the years go by? Is the Holy Spirit in charge of your tongue—do you try to comfort and build him up by what you say; or are you guilty, like so many of us, of the kind of verbal sniping which hurts more than any blow?

"Is it kind, is it true, is it necessary?" If we measured all our comments by this standard, far less would be said in many homes.

Now that you are a Christian there inevitably are some problems in your life that your husband finds difficult to appreciate. Accept that fact, but never build the beginning of a barrier between you by telling him that only So-and-so (another Christian) can possibly understand what is bothering you. If he is concerned because you are moody, admit that you are feeling down (there is no need to go into details), and draw strength and comfort from the love that prompted that concern. Remember that God Himself is the one completely unbiased and fully sympathetic listener, who is always available, even if all that you have to say is that you don't feel like praying! He may provide you with a wise and trustworthy Christian friend who can help and advise you with your problem. This can be an enormous help. But be sure when you tell something in confidence you refrain from the kind of gossip session which many women thrive on. Prayer requests can easily become character assassinations, so beware!

"Love is not jealous"—you know that and so do I! Yet jealousy can creep up on us almost unnoticed, causing many angry words and unhappy hours. It needs to be recognized for what it is—and dealt with. Can you be genuinely pleased when others succeed in a hobby or job—or do you feel let down and frustrated because your life seems dull by comparison? What about your husband's relationship with the children? How do you feel when he goes off with your son to a football game while you are left at home with the baby? Is it jealousy that makes you slam the kitchen door and shout at the cat? Or perhaps your daughter shows the sunny side of her character to her father so that you seem to be the only one who ever gets after her. Jealousy is fear— fear of being less loved, less wanted, less successful. "Perfect love casts out fear" (1 John 4:18). It is the perfect antidote for any jealous fear and uncertainty—apply it daily as required!

## Days of Small Things

"It's not very hard to be loving in the face of big problems. It's the little things that are so irritating —like water dripping and wearing away rock. It's not that Peter is anti-Christian exactly, but there are so many little details that we look at differently these days." Jane was still a new Christian and she was finding the going hard.

"Take television for instance. I don't mind watching it when there is something good on, but I hate coming in from church on Sunday evening to find it blaring away—it's like coming into another world. And the way Peter moans if I want to give some extra money to any Christian work while he spends more on records each month than I ever give! It's not fair! Then there's reading in bed. You wouldn't think that would be a problem, would you? But I like to read my Bible the last thing at night and it seems all wrong, me lying there reading my Bible while Peter is lying on the other side of the bed reading his thrillers. I'd burn them all if I was given half a chance."

"Why is it wrong?" asked Elizabeth, who was older in years and in the faith, and much wiser. "Peter is only behaving the way it is natural for him to behave. The same way you behaved until not so long ago. You are wrong, Jane, to expect him to behave like a Christian when he is not. It is quite natural that he wants to spend his money the way that pleases him. There's no need for you to feel guilty if you are not able to give as much to Christian work as you would like to. God knows your motives and how much you are keeping back for yourself, and that's what counts with Him. So don't nag Peter about his taste in television programs, books, or anything else. If you do, you are suggesting that you will love him only if he conforms to your standards. And without Jesus in his life he's got neither the motivation nor the power to do it."

"I suppose you're right," admitted Jane reluctantly, "but what can I do about bedtime? It's important to me. I want the Bible to be the last thing I read, so that it fills my mind as I go to sleep, and I know Peter doesn't like it much. Not that he says anything, but there's . . . well, an atmosphere."

"Put yourself in his position," Elizabeth suggested, "and it's not hard to see why. Peter probably thinks you're just doing it to impress him, and that immediately puts him on the defensive. How would you feel if he lay there reading *The Thoughts of Chairman Mao* and telling you that the novel that you were reading was an insult to the liberated mind of the common people! One way to solve this problem would be to memorize passages from the Bible. It is good to do anyway, and you could think over these verses the last thing at night without upsetting anyone.

"As for the television problem—stamps solved that for us. I didn't dream that this would happen when I started taking an interest in John's stamp collection—I just wanted to share his interests more. Then somehow Sunday evening after church has become the time we get the stamps out and the television goes on less and less frequently. Sometimes John wants to watch it, and then I ask God to keep the peace and joy of the service singing in my heart, and drown any feelings of resentment with His love—and He does."

## The Discipline of Love

"If you love someone, you will be loyal to him no matter what the cost. You will always believe in him, always expect the best of him, and always stand your ground in defending him" (1 Cor. 13:7, LB).

Is this another way of saying that love should ignore the faults in the beloved? "Love is blind," we say, but though this may be true of human love, it is never true of God's love. God loves us while knowing all about our failures, but in His love, He orders our circumstances so that we are disciplined and trained, and the failures and shortcomings which spoil our lives are gradually eradicated. God's all-accepting love is to be our standard.

No two people can live together within the intimacy of marriage without each one becoming all too aware of the other's faults. The trouble is that we are also all too ready to try and put each other straight. Though it may be right on some occasions to point out a fault or a mistake, think very carefully about your motives before you rush in. Read Galatians 6:1: "Brothers, if a man is trapped in some sin, you who are spiritual should restore him gently. But watch yourself; you also may be tempted" (NIV).

"You who are spiritual"—does this describe you or would "you who are glad to be right this time" be more appropriate? Are you gentle and humble? Have you been at fault in any way? Are you cherishing illusions about your own resistance to temptation? Is it necessary to say anything, or would it be better to pray, and let the Holy Spirit work?

Having thought and prayed through all these points, hand the whole matter over to Jesus. If it is His will for you to say anything to your husband, then He will give you the opportunity to speak gently and with His love. If that opening does not come—keep quiet. God has other plans, and He will accomplish them in His own way, however impossible this may seem to you.

## Love Never Ends
This kind of loving is not supposed to last for just a day or a week or a month, but forever. Do you feel that you could never keep it up on your own? You are quite right; you could not and neither could I. Jesus said, "Apart from Me you can do nothing" (John 15:5). But the wonderful thing is that you do not have to do it on your own. All you have to do is ask for His help day by day to keep the channel of your life whole, clean, and connected to the wellspring of His love. Given your obedience in this, the Holy Spirit can produce this fruit of love which will shine like a beacon in your small corner of God's world, and which nothing and nobody can put out.

# 8

## I'm a Failure

It's been one of those days! You woke up late feeling overwhelmed by the prospect of all you had to do, and from the moment you got out of bed everything seemed to go wrong. The children have been unmanageable, you've had a squabble with your husband, and by bedtime you have arrived at the conclusion that there is nothing in this Christianity business after all. The future stretches ahead in a series of gray monotonous days ending in futility. You don't even want to pray.

Have you had days or even weeks like that? There are few of us who have not. Perhaps life has not been particularly difficult, but the Bible seems as dry as dust and your prayers seem to get no higher than the ceiling. Doubts about your faith creep into your mind, and before long you wonder if you can possibly be a Christian at all if you feel like this. What is the remedy for times like these, and how should we apply it? It is hard to think rationally at times like that, but you must.

## Physical Causes

First of all it is important to recognize possible causes. One of the most frequent causes of feminine moodiness is the monthly ebb and flow of a woman's hormones. Much has been written on this subject, and there is no need to go into detail here, other than to say that the cause of premenstrual tension is not spiritual but physical, and the right steps to take, if it is very severe, are those in the direction of your doctor's office! So when you wake up feeling blue, check the calendar. If you can't blame it on your hormones, consider other physical causes. Would a few nights extra sleep or a little less dashing around during the day give you a different view of life?

## Spiritual Causes

If none of these simple, but often overlooked, causes apply to your "off-day," then it is time to dig a little deeper. Are you trying to live the Christian life in your own strength, struggling to break old habits and change yourself into a carbon copy of the Christian that you most admire? Then stop trying! It is a demoralizing struggle and what is more, it is a waste of time because it is impossible. The only person God wants you to be like is the Lord Jesus. Gradually, as we stop struggling to improve ourselves and let the Holy Spirit mold us into His pattern, we will reflect His likeness. Every time we obey His prompting, every time we allow Jesus' patient love to have the upper hand instead of our own irritable self-love, we take one step forward.

Even the difficult times of doubt and spiritual dryness can drive our roots down deeper into the love of God if we recognize them as disciplines to help, instead of demons to destroy.

But perhaps the underlying cause of your problem is something more specific. Are you worrying about anything, facing a problem with which you feel unable to cope? Paul has something to say about that: "Be anxious for nothing, but in everything by prayer and supplication with thanksgiving let your requests be made known to God. And the peace of God, which surpasses all comprehension, shall guard your hearts and minds in Christ Jesus" (Phil. 4:6).

Worry is disobedience, and as such is sin. Take your problem to Jesus, ask for His wisdom, and in faith thank Him for His help. Then take one positive step toward the solution. Treat it like a tree to be cut down. When lumberjacks are felling trees, they do not go straight to the main trunk and hack away with a saw or ax. Instead they trim off the small branches first, and then tackle the larger ones. Only when the twigs have been dealt with do they tackle the main trunk. So it is with any problem that defeats you. Ask Jesus to show you what small part can be dealt with right away. Lop that off and you will find that the whole thing seems a lot more manageable.

Maybe you are saying, "It would be simple if I knew why I felt like this, and then I could deal with it, but I don't." If this is the way you feel, ask the Holy Spirit to show you if there is something festering under the surface.

Do you look at other women and say to yourself, "I could be a radiant Christian like her if only

I was as calm as she is, or if I found it as easy to talk to people as she does. If only my children were still young enough to do as I say—or old enough to be out of my hair. If only Jim was like Steve, we would all be in church every Sunday—and if I had plenty of spare time like Sally I'd be a Sunday School teacher too." "If only, if only, if only" . . . don't waste your time in wishful thinking. God has given you your temperament, time, and talents. He has plans for your husband, your family, and your particular opportunities for serving Him—accept them gladly as His gifts. And in return give Him what He longs for most—yourself. Then all these other things will fit into place, and you will learn the lessons that will enable you to be His person in your unique situation.

These are the usual causes of spiritual despondency which attack us all from time to time. But sometimes we have to look outside ourselves and recognize that these difficult periods may be a direct attack of the devil, aimed at discouraging us and making us less useful in God's service. This often happens after a time when we have been on the crest of the wave spiritually. The Bible has a concise answer to that situation: "Resist the devil and he will flee from you" (James 4:7).

### The Sufficiency of Jesus

While it is occasionally necessary to take a spiritual inventory, don't brood; keep your eyes firmly fixed on Jesus. If you have Him you have all you need—claim Him, and enjoy your inheritance. Too many Christians are like the Texas rancher who used to ride over his ranch, worrying about how he was going to pay his bills. Little did he know that deep down under the surface of his land was an enormous oil field, which, once drilled, would make him a millionaire several times over. He owned the land and the undiscovered oilfield and yet he thought he was so poor that he was living on government assistance.

"My God shall supply all your needs" (Phil. 4:19) —do you believe it? Do you keep short accounts with God, asking for and accepting His forgiveness immediately when the Holy Spirit makes you conscious of some sin in your life? Or do you mope along feeling guilty and out of touch with God because you did the same thing today that you did yesterday, and you really can't expect Him to forgive you again? You might not expect it but you can accept it—"There is therefore now no condemnation for those who are in Christ Jesus" (Rom. 8:1). The voice that says there is comes straight from the devil.

How about your material needs? Do you believe that God will supply those? Notice that the word is *need*—not *want*. You are unlikely to find a mink coat in a box at your front door, but if for instance, like Carol, you needed gas or bus money to enable you to do some specific piece of Christian service you can trust Him to provide it. She did and was not disappointed. God's provision in material things is not limited to the George Muellers, Hudson Taylors, and Brother Andrews of this world.

"For a child will be given to us; and the government will rest upon His shoulders; and His name will be called Wonderful Counselor, Mighty God, Eternal Father, Prince of Peace" (Isa. 9:6). Is the government of your life on His shoulder? Then you can know Him in all these ways. Do you need wisdom? He is the wonderful counselor who will guide and patiently help you, no matter how slowly you learn.

Are there problems in your life for which none of your friends or professional advisers can offer solutions? You have the ear of the Mighty God, with whom all things are possible.

Do you ever get tired of being "Mom"—the one to whom everyone comes, expecting strength, confidence, and 24-hour availability? At those times you can turn to the Everlasting Father. Maybe your human parents are no longer available to ease some of the strains of life—lean back on the everlasting arms; they will never let you fall.

In a world full of tension and hatred, we have Jesus as Prince of Peace. Say these words over to yourself: If you have Him, you are living in the constant company of the Prince of Peace. Do you let His peace rule in your heart? Claim this on "one of those days" and though your circumstances may not change, there will be peace at the center of the storm.

So don't condemn yourself for your failures. Bring them to Jesus and claim His resources, remembering that you are, as E. Stanley Jones put it, "neither worm nor wonder, but a bundle of possibilities in Jesus Christ."

# 9

# At Home Where
# It's Hardest

It is harder to be a Christian at home than almost anywhere else. Most of us find it easy to put on our best behavior for the benefit of the rest of the world, but at home, where no one sees us but those who think nothing of showing us their less pleasant sides, it is a different matter. Those who see us everyday know what we really are.

The Bible holds up a very high standard for wives and homemakers. If you have read the description of the "virtuous woman" in Proverbs 31:10-31, you may have dismissed it as being written for another age. All this talk of rising "while it is yet night" and providing "food for her household and [prescribed tasks] for her maidens"—who has maids anymore? There is only one maid in our house and that is me. Surely it could not mean, in today's context, that she gets up on time, gets the wash going, and has an appetizing breakfast on the table for the family before they rush off to work and school . . . or could it?

## The Virtuous Woman

Take a closer look at the virtuous woman in a modern translation and you will find that she is very up-to-date. She is a business woman, a do-it-yourselfer; she helps those less fortunate than herself and is the inspiration and architect of her husband's success. If all that makes you want to creep away into the nearest corner and hide, take heart. Creating a home is a gradual process, and a homemaker grows along with it.

After all, your first home after you were married was probably very different from the one you live in today. And somewhere along the way you may have changed from "Can't-boil-an-egg Barbara" to "Souffles-are-simple Susie."

But the most important thing about a home in which Jesus has a part is not the furnishings or your accomplishments as a cook, but the atmosphere. What do you contribute to the atmosphere of your home? Dr. Norman Harrison compares the family circle to a wheel. Father is the rim forming a protective cushion between the family and the world, and mother is the hub—everything in the home revolves around her. If the hub is off-center the whole wheel is thrown off-balance. We can see how this works out. When you wake up in the morning, full of eager anticipation for the day ahead, the morning starts well for all the rest of the family. The reverse is equally true.

Does this mean that the atmosphere in your home is going to swing from happy to moody, from cheerful to silent in direct relationship to the way you feel? It can when we lose touch with Jesus Christ. But in Him there is stability. James said, "With [Him] there is no variation or shifting shadow" (1:17). The writer of Hebrews said, "Jesus Christ is the same yesterday, and today, yes, and for ever" (13:8). So if His life is flowing through you, you too can know the kind of inner peace and stability that is not disturbed by the winds of circumstance that may ruffle the surface of your life. Of course, this does not mean that the atmosphere of your home will be calm and peaceful when your husband has lost his car keys, your sons are quarreling ferociously over who owns a certain baseball card, and the toddler has dumped the remains of her cereal onto the kitchen floor (much to the delight of the cat). But it does mean that your whole day will not be ruined as you consciously put aside your irritation, and allow Jesus' peace and joy to have the upper hand.

## The Virtue of Gentleness

The Apostle Peter said, "Don't be concerned about the outward beauty that depends on jewelry, or beautiful clothes, or hair arrangement. Be beautiful inside, in your hearts, with the lasting charm of a gentle and quiet spirit which is so precious to God" (1 Peter 3:3-4, LB). Have you ever thought that this verse might apply to you? Sure—you have heard that Christian women should be more concerned with what goes on in their personalities than what they put on their faces! Carefully consider the phrase, "a gentle and quiet spirit." It came as a shock to me that this was a direct command— not just an optional extra for those who happened to be temperamentally suited to it!

So, if this is a command to be obeyed, how do we do it? As with everything in the Christian life, there are two parts to our obedience. First, the command itself; and second, the way it works out in our everyday lives.

What does having "a gentle and quiet spirit" involve? We have already thought of the way in which we can allow the love, peace, and serenity of Jesus to flow through us. Do we have to be wishy-washy and spineless to be calm and gentle? Not at all. (Sometimes children need to know in no uncertain terms that they have gone about as far as they can go.) Does it mean that we should "cop-out" and let the world pass us by, ignoring its problems? No, it does not.

## Fevers of the Spirit

Let's look at the question from a different angle. What in your life stops you from feeling calm, quiet, and gentle? A fever? I don't mean the kind of fever that sends the mercury rocketing up inside a thermometer, but the spiritual fever that damages our spiritual health and well-being. We could call one the fever of anxiety. Are you a worrier? What about fevers of resentment and rebellion? It only takes a few complaints of "It's not fair" or "I won't stand for that" before the fever takes over. Do you suffer from fevers of jealousy or self-pity—perhaps the most common there are? "Nobody understands what I have to put up with; everything falls back on me . . ."

And then there is busyness. Have you ever thought of that as a fever? It can be, on those days when the hands of the clock seem to move at twice their normal rate. Every job gets interrupted, and you madly hop around like the White Rabbit in *Alice in Wonderland,* muttering, "I'm late, I'm late, I'm late."

If left untreated, fevers can quickly progress into something more serious, so don't neglect them. What is the cure? Not a convenient bottle of medicine which you can keep on the shelf, but something even more effective.

"Now Simon's mother-in-law was lying sick with a fever . . . and [Jesus] came to her and raised her up, taking her by the hand, and the fever left her" (Mark 1:30-31). Of course, Simon's mother-in-law had a physical fever. But the touch of Jesus is just as effective on fevers of the spirit. So when you feel a spiritual fever coming on, stop and stretch out your hand to Jesus as you bring it to Him in prayer.

## Preventing Fevers

Of course, prevention is even better than a cure. Let's think about some practical steps that we can take, in partnership with the Holy Spirit, to stop fevers of the spirit from infecting us in the first place.

You can begin by organizing your weekly activities and responsibilities. You hate to be bound to a schedule? You feel it locks you into a routine? That's a possibility but all of us know how quickly minutes turn into hours, and hours into days, then into weeks. Without some effort on our part to regulate our use of time, the really important things get squeezed out.

Unless you are naturally a very methodical person you will probably find it helpful to make a rough daily schedule and an even rougher one for a week.

This does not mean that you are rigidly bound by that piece of paper to do the wash on Monday, even if it is pouring rain, and your shopping on Wednesday even if you have been invited over to a friend's house for coffee. But it does help you group your various jobs together and sort out your priorities.

Your first priority is to find time to spend with God. No matter how busy we are, unless we keep in touch with headquarters, neither we nor our families will grow and develop in the way He wants. Every other aspect of our lives will suffer as well.

Your next priority is the ordinary household jobs that are always there. Can you find a way of doing them more efficiently? Can you cut out some trips to the store by planning a week's worth of meals in advance and shopping accordingly? Have you got the will-power to discipline yourself and your family to straighten up their clutter as they go? It's an uphill struggle, but it will pay dividends in the long run.

Once you have made an attempt to get your daily work under control, can you be free enough from pressure to really listen to your children when they come home from school? Will you set aside some time in the day when your toddler can proceed at his own pace, without a constant stream of "Hurry, hurry, hurry!" from you? And what about some time for you to rest and relax? Everyone should have one period in the day which is his own, to do his own thing. You may have to cut down things that are good in themselves in order to fit that in, but don't feel guilty. It is almost impossible to have a "calm and gentle spirit" if you are exhausted because you never stop from morning to night. Often the best time to pause is when the pressure is at its peak. If you spend just ten minutes flopped in a chair or on the bed, consciously relaxing your tensed-up muscles and emptying your mind of racing thoughts, you will be repaid dividends. You don't believe it? Try it and you will be amazed at the results.

So plan your work, and follow your schedule. Remember that you share the yoke with Jesus and that His yoke is easy and His burden is light. Get into the habit of praying over problems as they arise. Discipline yourself to face one day at a time and refuse to let tomorrow's problems cloud today. As Paul said, "And now just as you trusted Christ to save you, trust Him, too, for each day's problems; live in vital union with Him" (Col. 2:16, LB). The psalmist said, "This is the day which the Lord has made, let us rejoice and be glad in it" (Ps. 118:24). Today's opportunities are unique, both to give and to get. This includes days when the going is easy, and days when everything seems too difficult for words. But each day can be faced in this spirit"— "If the Lord has allowed this I will be glad." This attitude is an act of the will and not of the emotions.

Paul puts it another way. "In everything give thanks; for this is God's will for you in Christ Jesus" (1 Thes. 5:18). This is the best preventive for spiritual fevers that I know. Note once again that it is a command; not an optional extra. Have you missed the bus? Give thanks; maybe the Lord has someone He wants you to meet as you wait at the bus stop or walk home. You can't go to that church service? Perhaps tonight will be the night that you can talk to your husband about Jesus.

Does this sound rather idealistic, almost unrealistic? Well, do you believe that "God causes all things to work together for good to those who love [Him] (Rom. 8:28)? In everything? If you do, giving thanks in every situation is totally realistic. What is more, it sets you free from fighting against circumstances and worrying that so easily takes over, so that you can live life at home with that "gentle and quiet spirit, which in God's sight is very precious."

Do you sometimes cry out with real longing, "Take from our lives the strain and stress, and let our ordered lives confess the beauty of Thy peace"? Well, it is not just a beautiful dream, it is a practical proposition. God is waiting to do it. Will you let Him?

# 10

# Bridge over
# Troubled Water

We hear a lot about the communication problem these days. Teenagers cannot communicate with their parents; parents lose touch with their married children. Even within the closest relationship of all we hear, "Bill and I have nothing to say to each other these days. We're just two people living in the same house."

Only last week, yet another marriage reached the divorce courts for this very reason—the husband could not or would not talk to his wife.

## What Is Communication?

What does the word *communicate* mean? *Webster's New Collegiate Dictionary* defines it like this: "To transmit information, thought, or feeling so that it is satisfactorily received or understood." This sounds simple enough on the surface, so why do so many people find it very hard, if not impossible, to share their thoughts and feelings with each other on any more than a superficial level? Whatever the reasons may be, the inability to communicate is the rock on which many relationships founder, and is a danger which needs to be faced and overcome.

Is it possible for "two to become one," which according to the Bible is God's plan for marriage (Matt. 19:5)? Yes, for "with God all things are possible," as Jesus said (19:26). But there is no such thing as "instant·togetherness" that slips on with the wedding rings. People grow together as they begin to know each other, and share experiences over the months and years of marriage. In addition to getting to know each other, you get to know yourself. How well did you know yourself before you became a wife and mother? Carol did not know that she had a temper until she had three children under two, who were in the habit of crying in time with each other at the most inconvenient moments! Margaret had no idea how much untidiness bothered her until she discovered that Jim dropped his clothes as he took them off—and left them where they fell!

The marriage service sets two people as a couple and as individuals off on a voyage of discovery which may go on throughout their lives, but all too often stops short because they are afraid. Afraid? Yes, afraid that if they reveal too much, they will hand over the weapon that can hurt them in their most sensitive spots. So, consciously or unconsciously they hold back something of themselves, in order to retain a safe place where no one can hurt them. And while they are doing this, true oneness is spoiled to a greater or lesser degree.

Is there a remedy? Yes, if you are willing to consider ourselves dead to the pride that insists that you keep up that protective pretense. When you say with Paul, "I have been crucified with Christ" (Gal. 2:20), you agree, among other things, to be crucified to all forms of pretense. You can be your true self with Jesus because He loves and accepts you as you are. As the light of His love shows you your faults and enables you to being working on them, you can learn to accept yourself and be open with others, giving love without self-seeking or withdrawing or holding back because you are afraid to be hurt.

Ask Jesus to give you His love this way. Communication is essentially a two-way street, but if even one of the people involved is ready to take this first step, then the vicious circle of "I won't . . . because he won't . . . because I won't . . ." is broken. Then you will be ready to take practical steps to help initiate real communication within your family situation.

## Unspoken Communication

Every marriage has a language of its own, one which is not dependent on words alone. A glance across a crowded room at a party can say, "This is fun, isn't it?" or "There's going to be trouble when we get home." The icy silence which envelopes many couples after an argument can carry on the battle just as viciously as words. A squeeze of the fingers as you wait in the hospital says all that is needed; a cheerful wave and a smile spells out, "Have a good day."

Actions say things too. What is the message that comes from a wife who only has time for what she wants to do, who goes out in the evening more often that she stays in, and consults her mother on every marital problem?

On the other hand, what are you saying when you substitute an evening at home for an evening out, because he is extra tired and is catching a cold? Or when you cook his favorite meal, or cheerfully switch on the football game instead of your favorite program?

Above and beyond all this is the most basic and important unspoken communication between husband and wife—the act of making love. Here, as in every other aspect of marriage, willingness to adapt to each other's needs is essential. The fact that two people are married is no guarantee that their need to express their love in physical terms will be the same, and in any case, this can vary in different circumstances. Worry, unhappiness, illness, and sheer physical fatigue can all affect a wife's responsiveness. The same is true for her husband. These problems will usually solve themselves, given time, but if they do not, or if the lack of physical harmony is due to deeper problems—resentment, misinformation during childhood, fear of pregnancy, or simply lack of knowledge—don't be afraid to ask for help.

Does it seem strange to suggest that you should pray about any problems that you may have in this sphere? God is interested in every aspect of your marriage, and He can give you insight into the cause of your difficulties as well as the grace to help you overcome them. Sometimes the answer is easy. Perhaps your problem is constant fatigue— you always fall asleep as soon as your head touches the pillow. If there is no apparent reason for this tiredness, see your doctor. It may be due to something as simple as mild anemia that some iron tablets would cure. If you know that you are simply doing too much, recognize the importance of the sexual aspect of your marriage and take steps to cut out something in your daily routine so you can get some rest.

Jenny was concerned because her and her husband's lovemaking became very routine. She prayed about it, and a few days later found a most helpful book on marriage in the public library, lodged rather unexpectedly between two books on theology in the philosophy section! She took it home; she and her husband both read it, and she returned it to the library. She has never seen it there since. A mere coincidence? Perhaps! Certainly the reading of a book did not in itself transform this area of their marriage, but recognizing the existence of a problem and taking practical steps to solve it made a great difference.

Mary's problem went deeper than boredom. She deeply resented her husband's refusal to take her Christian faith seriously, and almost without realizing it, was seeking to punish him by refusing to respond to his lovemaking. A talk with a Christian doctor helped her face up to the problem, and after a long inner struggle, confess it and ask for forgiveness.

Maybe none of these incidents parallel your situation, maybe you are disappointed because you have not experienced the ecstatic feelings portrayed as essential in some marriage manuals. Whatever the cause, this piece of advice can transform your attitude and with it reduce the problems: "Put your own needs on one side, and concentrate on giving love, and satisfying your partner. As you forget yourself and your feelings, you will find that you are able to receive as well."

Sounds too simple? We have thought about it before—the self-giving love, of Jesus. Ask Him for it in this situation and prove for yourself what a difference His love can make.

However vital actions may be, there comes a time when there is no substitute for words. The art of talking things over is the oil that keeps a marriage running smoothly. But if you want your talking to have the best results, ask the Holy Spirit to take control of your tongue, for talking in itself can sometimes do more harm than good.

## Do You Have Anything to Say?

What did you contribute to the conversation last night? Do you expect your husband to make up for the fact that he is out of the house all day and you are not, by having a fund of fascinating stories to bring home each evening? Or do you see that it is part of your responsibility to contribute to the suppertime conversation more than comments on the rising cost of meat and the children's mischief. Be selective—don't talk about your Christian activities until both of you are bored, but look for topics that interest you both.

Of course this will mean a deliberate effort on your part to keep up to date with the world around you. You may have to go more than halfway to find a hobby or interest that you can share. In your efforts to participate, remember that every conversation needs a talker and a listener and that you should take turns in both roles. When you listen, give your husband your full attention. You may be so used to giving half an ear to the children's chatter and thinking of other things at the same time that it has become a habit—a very exasperating one.

## How Do You Say It?

"It's not so much what you do and say, but the way you do and say it." Have you ever thought that the way in which you phrase a remark can make all the difference between harmony and discord? What effects do you think these two remarks would have on your husband?

"What do you mean? I'm not always dashing out in the evening. This is only the second time I've been out this week."

"Do you really feel that I am out too much in the evening? Well, how often do you feel is reasonable?"

The first remark sets the scene for a real yelling match; the second invites reasonable discussion in which each person's opinion counts. When the atmosphere is already stormy, phrase your remarks with care, and respect other people's rights to their own opinions—even if you are convinced that they are wrong!

## When Do You Say It?

Do you have a sense of timing? Many misunderstandings arise because we choose the wrong time to bring up a sticky subject. Steer away from unpleasant discussions when you are tired, hurried, or otherwise under stress. If your husband comes home tired and needing an extra helping of comfort and consolation, shelve the problems you were planning to discuss or the meeting that you were planning to attend, and turn your attention to his needs.

Are you available when he wants to talk? Are

you prepared to stay up late if necessary to welcome him home from a business trip? Do you put down your library book willingly to listen to what he has to say? And when he tells you something, can he be sure that it will go no further? Not even to your prayer group or to your Christian friend down the street? Do you make sure that you are at home together often enough to make conversation possible? If you do, then the battle is almost won. Sharing things together is becoming a habit, and that is a very good foundation for real communication.

## The Strong and Silent Type

It's surprising how often the heroes of romantic novels are portrayed as capable men of few words. Living with a man who is a "doer" rather than a "sayer" can bring very real complications into your relationship, as it emphasizes a basic difference between the sexes.

Most women love to talk. They are more ready to discuss their feelings and moods than men, and find it hard to understand that the majority of husbands, even the talkers, do not indulge in the verbal soul-searching and prolonged discussion of problems that wives enjoy. All of us need to ask the Holy Spirit to show us when to speak and when to keep silent. On the days when these differences in tempermental make-up irritate you, forget your grievances and look for the good points in your marriage partner. Think again about the little kindnesses that you take for granted. How long is it since you have said "thank you" and really meant it?

"Thank you" and "I love you" are five words that

need to be said every day. They help build an all-weather communication bridge between husband and wife which God can bless to make the bad times bearable and the good times glorious.

# 11

# Going Forward
# Together

"All right, I'll come to this service of yours, but after tonight I don't want to hear any more about this Christianity business! Enough is enough," he yelled.

With these harsh words ringing in her ears, Jenny started to church for her baptismal service, leaving Paul to follow later. Little did she imagine that that very evening Paul would be among those making their way to the front of the church as an indication that he, too, wanted to make a fresh start with Jesus Christ. At that time, Jenny had been a Christian for about two years.

Ann had to wait longer. For nine years she had to learn the lessons of faith and patience in God's school of waiting, while Mike's attitude toward her faith swung between bland indifference and downright disapproval. Through all the ups and downs she clung to the promise of this verse: "Delight yourself in the Lord; and He will give you the desires of your heart" (Ps. 37:4).

This was the assurance that had come to her as she prayed at the beginning of her Christian life that Mike would one day share her faith. She believed that that day would come, but it seemed to be slipping further and further into the future. As things got harder instead of easier, Mike's resistance toward Christianity and Ann's involvement in church life seemed to harden, so that when she was asked to help with the Sunday evening youth group, Mike wouldn't give it a hearing. (This was in spite of the fact that Ann had been a Sunday School teacher in the past with his full approval.) Symptoms of an old heart complaint returned and Mike could neither eat, sleep, nor concentrate on his job. Eventually he went to the doctor, only to be told that there was no physical cause for his symptoms.

Ann was wise enough to see the underlying spiritual battle in his moodiness and antagonism, and, though it was very difficult, she said little but prayed constantly as the Holy Spirit did His work. For several weeks Mike battled with his pride, refusing to admit that he had been wrong and fearing what commitment to Jesus Christ would mean to his way of life. At last the need for peace of mind pushed all these other considerations to one side, and Mike handed over the control of his life to Jesus during a church service.

This does not mean, of course, that the Holy Spirit can work only through a church service or after a set period of time. Don became a Christian just one month after his wife did, but while her church regarded her husband as a "hopeless case"

Mrs. Andrews waited twenty years before Bill came to share her faith.

There are no "hopeless cases" with God. Whether you are still looking forward to that day when you can live the Christian life with your husband, or whether you are taking your first steps together, you can trust Him all the way. Of course, it will make a difference, a wonderful difference in your life; things will need adjustment. Let's see how you can adapt to the changes that this longed-for event will bring.

## Think Back to Your Own Beginnings

Do you remember how you felt when you started out as a Christian? Were you a little confused, needing to think things through quietly, not sure what to read in the Bible or how to pray? Did you long for books to read that would explain the things you could not understand? Do you remember the time when much that you now take for granted was all new, exciting and perhaps a little strange?

This is where your husband is now. In your enthusiasm to share what you have learned, beware of swamping him with a second-hand faith. Offer advice and help only when it is asked for; be ready to share books that have helped you, but be selective. Match the books you offer to his needs. For example, a book on prayer written by a man would probably mean more to your husband than the "prayers from the kitchen sink" that have spoken to your heart so often.

Remember that God deals with us as individuals, so don't fall into the trap of comparing your husband's experience with your own. So what if you wanted to sing hymns from morning till night when you were a new Christian. That's great for you—but if your husband does not, that is fine too. He wants to tell everyone he meets about the wonderful change in his life? Be glad, but don't feel guilty because even now you find it difficult to talk to people about faith. God can meet your needs in this direction, just as He will meet your husband's need in another direction. The important thing is that you both recognize your own needs and bring them to God. You won't become perfect overnight and neither will your husband, so don't try to model your lives after each other, but be ready to help one another in every way that you can to become more and more like Jesus.

## Pray and Read the Bible Together

This is not a substitute for your own individual time with Jesus, but a wonderful bonus; a time in which the Holy Spirit can teach you together and open up a whole new area of communication as you learn to be more and more open with each other and with Him.

There is an emphasis here on learning—it does not happen all at once. Remember that as a new Christian your husband may find some parts of the Bible easier to understand and more applicable to his present experience than others. So start off with a Gospel like John or Mark for your joint reading rather than your favorite minor prophet. You may prefer to use a book like *Daily Light*, which has a selection of related verses for each day of the year. When it comes to discussing it afterwards, don't expect to have all the answers. The Holy Spirit may well reveal something to your husband that you have never noticed—so be prepared to learn from God's Word together.

Praying aloud is one hurdle that some Christians take in stride, while others never attempt it. Both Ann and Mike felt that God was prompting them to pray together and yet they found it impossible. Mike felt self-conscious at the thought of voicing a prayer that might not "sound right." Ann found herself completely tongue-tied when it came to praying aloud with the person who knew her best —though she had often prayed with her friends.

The situation might have gone on for months if they had not mentioned their difficulty to their minister. He visited in their home, and having talked to them about the various aspects of prayer, suggested that they pray together before he left.

"I'll pray first, then Mike can come in, and Ann can finish up."

Those first prayers were faltering and short. They were not full of long words or holy language, but they were sincere. God heard them, and as they came to Him for help the barrier was broken down. Since then, Ann and Mike have prayed together every day, and they are gradually learning to bring everything, even their own faults and failings, together to God in prayer.

Do you still feel that this could not work in your situation? That it is too difficult for two shy people like you? God can iron out these difficulties if you are willing to ask Him and then to do what He tells you. If you have never started to pray together, ask the Holy Spirit to put the desire to do so into both of your hearts and move on from there as He makes the opportunity.

Even when that is taken care of don't expect

praying together to always be easy, even when you have been doing it for years. Sometimes a resentment or a grudge has to be brought out, or a difference of opinion made up before you can pray at all. If you are really mad at him, or not speaking to him at all, you certainly cannot pray with him! The devil may discourage you by seeing to it that your prayer time is interrupted by the telephone ringing or the baby crying; often you may be too tired to feel like praying, but keep at it anyway. Real open-hearted prayer can cement the bonds of a marriage in a way that nothing else can do, so give it the place in your life together that God wants it to have.

## Throw Away Your Blueprint

In your daydreams of the wonderful day when your husband shared your faith, did you paint a glowing picture of exactly how he would behave—based on all your favorite characteristics of the Christian men you knew?

Did you think that he would have the biblical knowledge of David, lead family prayers like Roger, preach like Tony, be the first to put his hand in his pocket for church needs like John, and never miss a service like Peter? You did—with a lot of other things beside? Then throw away that blueprint quickly, before you are tempted to try to force your man into that mold and make one of the biggest mistakes of your life. Praise God for the man He has linked your life with—just as he is. In God's own time He may call your husband to preach or take a leading part in church affairs, but first he has to grow as a Christian. And he will grow according to God's pattern, not yours.

People are like plants; they all have their individual growth rates. No amount of anxious watching over them will make them grow faster. Of course, you will want to consider together how you should give to God's work, but give your husband time to learn about the principle of tithing before you wave a pledge card under his nose. Encourage him to take his place in the church family but don't try to rush him into church membership before he feels that he is ready, or into church work before he has gotten on his feet as a Christian.

On the other hand, avoid being over-protective. Don't shield him from the pressure that God intends to use to help him grow. There is no need for you to watch over him like a mother hen, "Oh no, I don't think you should ask Ben to read the Scripture passage this evening—he's never read the Bible in public before."

So what? There's a first time for everyone! Maybe this is not the time for Ben to start, but stand back and let him decide for himself when the Holy Spirit is leading him on to do something new.

Maybe it's in family matters that you will have to learn to "let go and let God." Remember that, although your husband may be a new Christian, in God's ordering of things he is still the leader in your marriage and has the responsibility for ordering the spiritual affairs of the home. Keep your hands off the reins and let him lead, however hesitant he may be at first.

Pray about these matters with him, of course. Give advice if he asks for it, and then as he takes each new step be generous with your praise, encouragement and, most of all, prayer.

So don't nag, criticize, or pamper your husband, but pray for him constantly, confident that the God who has called you both to Himself will lead you on "to help you understand what He wants you to do . . . to make you wise about spiritual things . . . that the way you live will always please the Lord and honor Him, that you will always be doing good kind things for others while all the time you are learning to know God better and better . . . praying too, that you will be filled with His mighty, glorious strength so that you can keep going no matter what happens—always full of the joy of the Lord, and always thankful to the Father who has made us fit to share all the wonderful things that belong to those who live in the kingdom of light" (Col. 1:9-12, LB).